by Iain Gray

Lang**Syne**

PUBLISHING

WRITING *to* REMEMBER

Lang**Syne**

PUBLISHING

WRITING *to* REMEMBER

79 Main Street, Newtongrange,
Midlothian EH22 4NA
Tel: 0131 344 0414   Fax: 0845 075 6085
E-mail: info@lang-syne.co.uk
www.langsyneshop.co.uk

Design by Dorothy Meikle
Printed by Ricoh Print Scotland
© Lang Syne Publishers Ltd 2015

ISBN 978-1-85217-645-7

Stewart

MOTTO:
Courage grows strong at a wound.

CREST:
A pelican in her nest, feeding her young.

NAME variations include:
Steuart
Stuart

Chapter one:

The origins of popular surnames

by George Forbes and Iain Gray

If you don't know where you came from, you won't know where you're going is a frequently quoted observation and one that has a particular resonance today when there has been a marked upsurge in interest in genealogy, with increasing numbers of people curious to trace their family roots.

Main sources for genealogical research include census returns and official records of births, marriages and deaths – and the key to unlocking the detail they contain is obviously a family surname, one that has been 'inherited' and passed from generation to generation.

No matter our station in life, we all have a surname – but it was not until about the middle of the fourteenth century that the practice of being identified by a particular surname became commonly established throughout the British Isles.

Previous to this, it was normal for a person to be identified through the use of only a forename.

But as population gradually increased and there were many more people with the same forename, surnames were adopted to distinguish one person, or community, from another.

Many common English surnames are patronymic in origin, meaning they stem from the forename of one's father – with 'Johnson,' for example, indicating 'son of John.'

It was the Normans, in the wake of their eleventh century conquest of Anglo-Saxon England, a pivotal moment in the nation's history, who first brought surnames into usage – although it was a gradual process.

For the Normans, these were names initially based on the title of their estates, local villages and chateaux in France to distinguish and identify these landholdings.

Such grand descriptions also helped enhance the prestige of these warlords and generally glorify their lofty positions high above the humble serfs slaving away below in the pecking order who had only single names, often with Biblical connotations as in Pierre and Jacques.

The only descriptive distinctions among the peasantry concerned their occupations, like 'Pierre the swineherd' or 'Jacques the ferryman.'

Roots of surnames that came into usage in England not only included Norman-French, but also Old French, Old Norse, Old English, Middle English, German, Latin, Greek, Hebrew and the Gaelic languages of the Celts.

The Normans themselves were originally Vikings, or 'Northmen', who raided, colonised and eventually settled down around the French coastline.

The had sailed up the Seine in their longboats in 900AD under their ferocious leader Rollo and ruled the roost in north eastern France before sailing over to conquer England in 1066 under Duke William of Normandy – better known to posterity as William the Conqueror, or King William I of England.

Granted lands in the newly-conquered England, some of their descendants later acquired territories in Wales, Scotland and Ireland – taking not only their own surnames, but also the practice of adopting a surname, with them.

But it was in England where Norman rule and custom first impacted, particularly in relation to the adoption of surnames.

This is reflected in the famous *Domesday Book*, a massive survey of much of England and Wales, ordered by William I, to determine who owned what, what it was worth and therefore how much they were liable to pay in taxes to the voracious Royal Exchequer.

Completed in 1086 and now held in the National Archives in Kew, London, 'Domesday' was an Old English word meaning 'Day of Judgement.'

This was because, in the words of one contemporary chronicler, "its decisions, like those of the Last Judgement, are unalterable."

It had been a requirement of all those English landholders – from the richest to the poorest – that they identify themselves for the purposes of the survey and for future reference by means of a surname.

This is why the *Domesday Book*, although written in Latin as was the practice for several centuries with both civic and ecclesiastical records, is an invaluable source for the early appearance of a wide range of English surnames.

Several of these names were coined in connection with occupations.

These include Baker and Smith, while Cooks, Chamberlains, Constables and Porters were to be found carrying out duties in large medieval households.

The church's influence can be found in names such as Bishop, Friar and Monk while the popular name of Bennett derives from the late fifth to mid-sixth century Saint Benedict, founder of the Benedictine order of monks.

The early medical profession is represented by Barber, while businessmen produced names that include Merchant and Sellers.

Down at the village watermill, the names that cropped up included Millar/Miller, Walker and Fuller, while other self-explanatory trades included Cooper, Tailor, Mason and Wright.

Even the scenery was utilised as in Moor, Hill, Wood and Forrest – while the hunt and the chase supplied names that include Hunter, Falconer, Fowler and Fox.

Colours are also a source of popular surnames, as in Black, Brown, Gray/Grey, Green and White, and would have denoted the colour of the clothing the person habitually wore or, apart from the obvious exception of 'Green', one's hair colouring or even complexion.

The surname Red developed into Reid, while

Blue was rare and no-one wanted to be associated with yellow.

Rather self-important individuals took surnames that include Goodman and Wiseman, while physical attributes crept into surnames such as Small and Little.

Many families proudly boast the heraldic device known as a Coat of Arms, as featured on our front cover.

The central motif of the Coat of Arms would originally have been what was borne on the shield of a warrior to distinguish himself from others on the battlefield.

Not featured on the Coat of Arms, but highlighted on page three, is the family motto and related crest – with the latter frequently different from the central motif.

Adding further variety to the rich cultural heritage that is represented by surnames is the appearance in recent times in lists of the 100 most common names found in England of ones that include Khan, Patel and Singh – names that have proud roots in the vast sub-continent of India.

Echoes of a far distant past can still be found in our surnames and they can be borne with pride in commemoration of our forebears.

Chapter two:

Anglo-Saxons and Normans

An occupational surname that from the fourteenth century became associated with an illustrious line of monarchs, 'Stewart' and its French spelling variant 'Stuart' is particularly identified with Scotland – although it is also prevalent throughout England, being ranked at 61st in some lists of the 100 most common surnames found there today.

Also a popular forename, it derives from the Old English ''stigweard' – from 'stig' meaning 'household' and 'weard' indicating 'guardian' – and hence the occupational designation of 'guardian of the house.'

The 'guardian' in question would have been someone entrusted with administering the domestic affairs of an ecclesiastical, noble or royal household, while 'stigweard' developed through time into the form 'steward' – with 'Stewart' becoming the surname of those employed as 'stewards.'

The Old English roots of the name indicates

that flowing through the veins of many bearers of the name today may well be the blood of those Germanic tribes who invaded and settled in the south and east of the island of Britain from about the early fifth century.

Known as the Anglo-Saxons, they were composed of the Jutes, from the area of the Jutland Peninsula in modern Denmark, the Saxons from Lower Saxony, in modern Germany and the Angles from the Angeln area of Germany.

They held sway in what became known as England from approximately 550 to 1066 – the year of the Norman Conquest of England – with the main kingdoms those of Sussex, Wessex, Northumbria, Mercia, Kent, East Anglia and Essex.

Duke William of Normandy was declared king of England after his victory over the last of the Anglo-Saxon kings, Harold II, at the battle of Hastings in 1066, and the complete subjugation of his Anglo-Saxon subjects followed.

Those Normans and others who had fought on his behalf were rewarded with the lands of Anglo-Saxons, while within an astonishingly short space of time, Norman manners, customs and law were imposed on England – laying the basis for what subsequently became established 'English' custom and practice.

But it is not only the blood of the Anglo-Saxons that flows through the veins of some bearers of the name today, but also that of the Normans and others such as Flemish and Breton knights who supported William in his conquest.

Among them was a knight who hailed from Dol, in Brittany, in northern France.

It is not known with any degree of certainty exactly where in England he was granted lands but, in the form of 'de Stiward' however, the name is recorded in the early years of the 12th century in Devon – and it is therefore with this modern-day English county that the name has a particular connection.

Meanwhile the family name of the Breton knight who was granted lands after the Conquest is believed to have been 'Dapifer', while his descendants later assumed the surname 'Fitz Alan', or 'Fitz Alain', and it is was one of these 'Fitz Alans' – Walter Fitz Alan – who became the progenitor of those who would assume the Stewart name in Scotland and, later, in England.

Along with other ambitious nobles, Walter Fitz Alan came north to Scotland during the reign from 1124 to 1153 of David I, the Scottish king having become enamoured by Norman customs and manners.

Fitz Alan and other nobles – such as the 'de Bruces', or 'Bruces' – were granted lands in some of the more unruly parts of David's kingdom in return for helping to quell unrest and assert his royal authority .

Walter Fitz Alan achieved high office under David, being appointed High Steward, or Great Steward of Scotland – the most powerful post in the land and placing him second in importance to the king himself.

With responsibility for not only administrative but also military affairs, he was granted lands in Renfrewshire and East Lothian, while his descendants – having adopted the surname 'Stewart' because the post of High Steward was hereditary – came to acquire other territory in Cowal, Bute, Arran and Kintyre.

It was through one of Walter's descendants, Walter Stewart, 6th High Steward of Scotland, that the royal dynasty of Stewart, or Stuart, was established – one that would rule from the early seventeenth century until the early eighteenth century over the kingdoms of not only Scotland but also England and Ireland.

This was through his marriage in 1315 – a

year after the warrior king Robert the Bruce's victory over the English army of Edward II at the battle of Bannockburn – to the king's only daughter, Marjorie.

When Bruce, recognised as Robert I, died in 1329, he was succeeded by his son Robert as Robert II. When his successor, David II, died in 1371, he was succeeded by Walter Stewart and Marjorie's son Robert, as Robert III.

A succession of Stewart Scottish monarchs followed, and it was in 1603, a key date in the history of both Scotland and England, that the fate of both nations became inextricably entwined.

This was when, following the death in January of that year of England's last Tudor monarch, Elizabeth I, James VI of Scotland succeeded to the English throne as James I.

Chapter three:

Union of crowns

From 1603 onwards, the history of the Stewarts in England is largely that of the royal dynasty of the name.

Born in Edinburgh Castle in 1566, the son of the ill-fated Mary, Queen of Scots and her dissolute husband Lord Darnley, James Stewart, whose accession to the English throne brought about the Union of the Crowns of Scotland and England, had been only one-year-old when his mother was forced to abdicate in his favour.

She had inherited the throne and the troubled realm of Scotland when she was only an infant, following the death of her father James V in December of 1542.

With her mother, Mary of Guise, ruling as regent, she was sent for her own safety at the age of six to the French royal court.

It is from about this period that the 'Stuart' spelling of the name became almost interchangeable with that of 'Stewart', the letter 'w' not being indigenous to the French language.

Mary married Francis, the French Dauphin, in April of 1558, just over a year before he succeeded to the French throne following the death of his father Henry II.

The young Mary was widowed in December of 1560 and she returned to Scotland to take up her throne. But by the time she returned, her realm was in the uncompromising grip of a religious reformation whose stern adherents distrusted her Catholicism.

This resulted in a series of tragic events that included the murder of her Italian secretary David Rizzio, the murder of her second husband Lord Darnley and her enforced abdication and flight in 1568 into English exile – where she naively thought she would be protected by Queen Elizabeth, her cousin.

Imprisoned after crossing the border, it ended with her falling victim to the executioner's axe in the Great Hall of Fotheringhay Castle, Northamptonshire after being found guilty on the basis of trumped-up charges of supporting a Catholic plot to overthrow Elizabeth in her favour.

It is therefore rather ironical that it was her son James who succeeded Elizabeth – the monarch who had signed his mother's death warrant.

His entitlement to the throne, which made

him master of the three kingdoms of Scotland, England and Ireland, came about because not only was he the son of Mary, Queen of Scots, but also a great-great-grandson of Henry VII.

Accompanied by his courtiers and other assorted hangers-on, James made his stately progress throughout England to take up his throne.

Although he had promised to visit Scotland at least every three years, he did so only once, in 1617, as he became firmly ensconced in his English court.

The first years of his reign as James I were not without controversy, with many English nobles jealous over what they perceived as the preferential treatment given by the king to the Scots who flocked to his court to seek advancement.

The Scots who had originally accompanied the king south had been perceived as ill-bred, uncouth and unclean and one lampoon of the time snidely noted that:

> *Thy sword at thy back was a great black blade,*
> *With a great basket-hilt of iron made*
> *But now a long rapier doth hang by his side,*
> *And huffingly doth this bonny Scot ride.*
> *Bonny Scot, we all witness can*
> *That England hath made thee a gentleman.*

It was only two years into his reign that the Protestant James I became the target of the infamous Gunpowder Plot.

This was when a number of disaffected Roman Catholic gentry, whose agent was Guido (Guy) Fawkes, made an abortive attempt to blow up the king, the Lords and the Commons at the formal opening of Parliament on November 5, 1605.

This plot to assassinate the first Stewart monarch of England is now commemorated annually as Guy Fawkes Night, or Bonfire Night.

James's 22-year reign is known as the Jacobean era, and it saw a great flourishing of the arts.

The king himself, given the rather back-handed compliment of being described as "The Wisest Fool in Christendom", not only sponsored the translation of the Bible known as the *Authorised King James Version*, but also penned a number of works that include his 1598 *True Law of Free Monarchies* and the 1599 manual on kingship *Basilikon Doron – Royal Gift*.

Through his marriage in 1589 to Anne of Denmark, he had three children who survived into adulthood.

They were Henry Frederick, Prince of Wales,

who died when aged 18, Elizabeth, later Queen of Bohemia and his successor the ill-fated Charles I, who was born in 1600.

Charles incurred the wrath of Parliament by his insistence on the 'divine right' of monarchs – a theme emphasised in his father's *Basilikon Doron* – and added to this was Parliament's fear of Catholic 'subversion' against the state and the king's stubborn refusal to grant demands for religious and constitutional concessions.

Matters came to a head with the outbreak of the English Civil War in 1642, with Parliamentary forces, known as the New Model Army and commanded by Oliver Cromwell and Sir Thomas Fairfax, arrayed against the Royalist army of the king.

In what became an increasingly bloody and complex conflict, spreading to Scotland and Ireland and with rapidly shifting loyalties on both sides, Charles I was led to the executioner's block in January of 1649 on the orders of Parliament.

He was succeeded by his son Charles, who was proclaimed King Charles II in Edinburgh and Dublin following his father's execution.

Invading England at the head of a Scots army, he was roundly defeated by Cromwell at the battle of Worcester in September of 1651, famously having to hide from his pursuers for a time in the branches of the 'royal oak' at Boscobel, Shropshire.

Escaping to the Continent, he returned to England on the Restoration of 1660.

Married to Catherine of Braganza, he never had any legitimate children, while he had a number of mistresses who included Eleanor ('Nell') Gwynn and Lucy Walter, mother of James Scott, Duke of Monmouth. He died in 1685, having declared himself a Catholic as he lay on his deathbed, and was succeeded by his brother James, Duke of York, as James II.

Born in 1633, this Stewart monarch, also known as James VII of Scotland, was the last Catholic monarch to reign over what became, after the Act of Union of 1707, Great Britain.

It was when his Catholic son and heir, also named James, was born in 1688 that Protestant unrest reached crisis point and leading English nobles invited William of Orange and his wife Mary – ironically a daughter of the king – to jointly take up the throne.

In what is known as the Glorious Revolution of 1688, James fled into exile in France and William and Mary took up the throne as William III and Mary II after arriving unopposed from Holland.

James, however, still had significant support in Ireland, and with the support of troops and money supplied by Louis XIV of France, he landed at Kinsale in March of 1689 and joined forces with his Irish supporters.

A series of military encounters followed, culminating in his defeat by an army commanded by William at the battle of the Boyne on July 12, 1689; James fled again into French exile, never to return.

Mary II, meanwhile, died in 1694 and William III in 1702.

He was succeeded by his sister-in-law Ann, who was married to Prince George of Denmark. The last of the Stewart/Stuart monarchs, she died childless in 1714 and under the Act of Settlement was succeeded by George I of Hanover, her second cousin and a descendant of the Stewarts through his maternal grandmother Elizabeth, a daughter of James I.

Supporters of the Stewart cause were known as Jacobites – after 'James' – and after the Hanoverian Succession their attention focussed on James Francis Edward Stuart, the son of the deposed James II and who had been living in exile.

Known as "The Old Pretender" or "The King Over the Water", it was in his name that in September of 1715 the Scottish Earl of Mar raised the Stuart Standard at Braemar.

He managed to muster a force of no less than 10,000 fighting men, but the Jacobite cause was effectively lost after the battle of Sheriffmuir, in November of 1715, when Mar withdrew his forces north to Perth.

James, the de facto James III of England and James VIII of Scotland, landed at Peterhead in Scotland in December, and then moved on to Perth, only to depart forever from Scottish shores in February of 1716.

The Rising had fizzled out, but the Stuart Standard was raised again more than thirty years later when James's son, Prince Charles Edward Stuart, known to his detractors as "The Young Pretender", arrived at the small Outer Hebridean island of Eriskay on July 22, 1745, landing on the mainland at Loch nan Uamh three days later.

The Stuart Standard was raised on August 19, at Glenfinnan, on Loch Shiel.

A victory over a Hanoverian army was achieved at the battle of Prestonpans in September, and in the following month the confident prince and his army set off on the long march south to London to claim what was believed to be the rightful Stuart inheritance of the throne.

But they reached only as far as Derby before the controversial decision was taken in early December to withdraw back over the border.

Jacobite hopes were then dashed forever on April 16, 1746 at the battle of Culloden, fought on Drummossie Moor, near Inverness – the last major battle fought on British soil and where the Jacobites were soundly defeated by a Hanoverian army.

Managing to evade his pursuers after the battle, the Prince – who had been the last hope of ardent supporters of the Stewart/Stuart cause – was eventually able to reach French shores, dying in lonely and embittered exile in Rome in 1788.

Chapter four:

On the world stage

Named by the American Film Institute as the third greatest male screen legend in cinema history, James Maitland Stewart, better known as James Stewart and, fondly, as Jimmy Stewart, was the actor who starred in a number of iconic Hollywood films.

Born in 1908 in Indiana, Pennsylvania, of Scottish and Irish ancestry, his father ran a hardware business that had been in the family for three generations.

His father's hope had been that his son would follow him in the business, but the lure of the stage proved too strong.

It was while attending Princeton University and studying architecture that he performed in its music and drama club, his musical speciality being the accordion.

Invited to join an inter-collegiate group known as the University Players, who performed during the summer months in West Falmouth, Massachusetts, on Cape Cod, Stewart came to the attention of the actor Henry Fonda, who also had performed with the University Players and who encouraged him to take up acting as a full-time career.

Following his advice, he appeared in a number of stage productions until, in 1935, he attracted the attention of MGM who signed him up as a contract player.

A number of small film roles followed, but his down-to-earth personality and distinctive drawl appealed to the movie-going public and his first major success was in the 1936 *After the Thin Man* followed, in the same year, in the romantic comedy *Next Time We Love*.

Dating actresses Ginger Rogers and then Norma Shearer for a brief period, further film success followed with *You Can't Take It With You*, winner of the 1938 Academy Award for Best Picture, the 1939 *Mr Smith Goes to Washington* – for which he was nominated for what would be the first of five Academy Awards throughout his career for Best Actor and the 1940 *The Philadelphia Story*.

Co-starring with Katharine Hepburn, this film won him an Academy Award for Best Actor.

Stewart had always been interested in flying, gaining his private pilot licence certificate in 1935 and, following America's entry into the Second World

War, he enlisted in the United States Army Air Force (USAAF) – being assigned in 1943 to the 445th Bomb Group as operations officer of the 703rd Bombardment Squadron.

His squadron flew to England and, based at RAF Tibenham, Norfolk, he flew on a number of bombing missions over Germany that included leading the 2nd Combat Bombardment Wing in an attack on Berlin in March of 1944.

Awarded the Distinguished Flying Cross on two occasions, the Air Medal and the Croix de Guerre, at the end of the conflict he continued to play a role in the United States Air Force Reserve – not retiring until 1968, with the rank of Brigadier General.

Back on the stage, he enjoyed success with a string of other films.

Most notably these include the 1946 *It's A Wonderful Life*, the 1950 *Harvey*, the 1954 *The Glenn Miller Story* and, directed by Alfred Hitchcock, the 1954 *Rear Window* and, from 1958, *Vertigo*.

Awarded the New York Film Critics Circle Award for Best Actor for his role in the 1959 *Anatomy of a Murder*, other films included the 1957 *The Spirit of St Louis*, the 1965 *The Flight of the Phoenix* and, co-starring with John Wayne, the 1976 *The Shootist*.

Married in 1949 to the former model Gloria McLean until her death in 1994 and the recipient of an Academy Lifetime Achievement Award, he died in 1997.

The son of a science teacher, Andrew Stewart, better known as **Andy Stewart**, was the actor, singer and all-around entertainer born in Glasgow in 1933.

Moving with his family to Arbroath, in the northeast of Scotland, when he was six, he first took to the stage at 16 in a church pageant – although from an early age he had entertained family and friends with his talent for impersonations of famous actors and singers.

Abandoning plans to pursue a career as a veterinary surgeon and deciding to become an actor, he enrolled at the Royal Scottish Academy of Music and Drama where, in his first year, he won its First Prize for Comedy.

Embarking on a career in the style of a music hall entertainer, he became famed for a string of hit songs that included the 1961 *Scottish Soldier*, *Come-In-Come-In*, *Campbeltown Loch*, *The Road to Dundee* and his self-penned *Donald Where's Your Troosers?*

The kilted entertainer was the compere of BBC Scotland's annual New Year's Eve, or Hogmanay, party *The White Heather Club* from 1957 to 1968.

From 1960 till 1968 he compered the equally popular weekly early evening series of *The White Heather Club*.

He died in 1993, having also starred in the Scottish Television series *Scotch Corner* and on Grampian Television's *Andy's Party* series.

He was the father of the stage, television and film actor **Andrew Ewan Stewart**, born in Glasgow in 1957.

His television credits include *Only Fools and Horses*, in the role of Dr Robbie Meadows, while film credits include the 1997 *Titanic* in the role of First Officer Murdoch.

On the television screen, **Alastair Stewart**, born in 1952 in Gosport, Hampshire and of Scottish and English parentage, is the journalist and newscaster who, after having worked for *Southern Television* and *Channel 4 News*, is now a main newsreader for *ITV News*.

The recipient of an OBE and having worked on local and national news for 38 years, he is the longest serving male newsreader on British television.

Behind the camera lens, **Robert Banks Stewart** is the scriptwriter born in Edinburgh in 1931.

A former journalist, he is known for an impressive body of work that includes scripts for popular television series from the 1950s onwards such as *Danger Man*, *The Avengers*, *Callan*, *The Sweeney*, *Shoestring*, *Bergerac* and *The Darling Buds of May*.

On American shores, **Donald Ogden Stewart** was the American author and screenwriter who won an Academy Award for his work on *The Philadelphia Story*; born in 1894 in Columbus, Ohio, he died in 1980.

From the stage to the world of music, Roderick David Stewart is the British rock singer and songwriter better known as **Rod Stewart**.

Born in 1945 in Highgate, North London to a Scottish father and an English mother and having to date sold more than 100 million records worldwide, he is recognised as one of the best-selling artists of all time.

Leaving school when aged 15, he worked in a number of jobs that included labouring in Highgate Cemetery, sign writing and fence erecting.

Encouraged by his father, his first ambition

was to become a professional footballer – and although this did not come to pass, he remains a passionate devotee of the game to this day, supporting both the Scottish national team and Scottish Premier League club Celtic.

His first foray into music came when he was aged 16 with a band called The Raiders, but it was not until the late 1960s – by this time having adopted what was known as 'Mod' fashion and with his 'trademark' spiky hair that 'Rod the Mod' came to prominence.

With his instantly recognisable raspy voice, he played with The Jeff Beck Group and The Faces until releasing his debut solo album, *An Old Raincoat Won't Ever let You Down*, in 1969.

Other albums include *A Night on the Town*, while internationally best-selling singles include *Maggie May*, *Sailing*, *Tonight's the Night*, *The First Cut is the Deepest*, *You're in my Heart*, *Hot Legs* and *Da Ya Think I'm Sexy?*

In addition to receiving a star on the Hollywood Walk of Fame, his many other honours and accolades include a CBE for services to music and induction into the Rock and Roll Hall of Fame and the UK Music Hall of Fame.

Born in Sunderland in 1952, David Allan Stewart, better known as **Dave Stewart**, is the English musician, songwriter and record producer who, along with Scots singer and musician Annie Lennox, enjoyed success as the duo Eurythmics – with hit singles that include *Sweet Dreams (Are Made of This)*.

Bearers of the Stewart name have also excelled in the highly competitive world of sport.

On the motor racing circuit, John Young Stewart, better known as **Jackie Stewart** and more formally as Sir Jackie Stewart, is the Scottish former Formula One driver born in 1939 in Milton, West Dunbartonshire.

Nicknamed "The Flying Scot", he competed in Formula One between 1965 and 1973, winning three World Drivers' Championships.

Winner in 1973 of BBC Television's Sports Personality of the Year and the recipient of a knighthood in 2001 he is now a commentator on the sport for American television.

He the father of **Paul Stewart** who, born in Dumbarton in 1965 and also a former racing driver, is now a television and film producer.

From the motor racing circuit to the golf course, William Payne Stewart, better known as

Payne Stewart, was the American professional golfer born in 1957 in Springfield, Missouri.

Known for his flamboyant dress style on the golf course, often incorporating brightly coloured 'knickerbocker' trousers, he won eleven Professional Golf Association (PGA) Tour events.

His last major championship win was the 1999 U.S. Open – sadly, a few months later the popular golfer was killed in an aeroplane crash.

On a rather macabre note, Robert Leslie Stewart, born in Edinburgh in 1918, and better known as **Jack Stewart**, was one of the last executioners in the United Kingdom, active in the role from 1950 until the suspension of capital punishment for murder in 1965.

He completed what was known as the Prison Commissioners' Assistant Executioner training course at Pentonville Prison, London.

As an assistant, he carried out 21 executions while in 1957 he was promoted to the post of executioner following the resignation of the executioner Albert Pierrepoint.

Immigrating to Australia after the abolition of capital punishment and taking up an entirely different career in the aircraft industry, he died in 1989.